Social Studies Alive!™

Our Community and Beyond

Teachers' Curriculum Institute

Bert Bower   Jim Lobdell

Managing Editor: Laura M. Alavosus
Production Editor: Mali Apple
Editorial Assistant: Anna Embree
Art Director: Tim Stephenson
Production Coordinator: Lynn Sanchez
Senior Graphic Designer: Christy Uyeno
Graphic Designers: Katy Haun, Victoria Philp,
    Paul Rebello
Photographer: Tim Stephenson
Photo Acquisitions: Anna Embree
Audio and Photography Director: Katy Haun
Operations Manager: Ellen Mapstone

This book is published by Teachers' Curriculum Institute.

 Teachers' Curriculum Institute
PO Box 50996
Palo Alto, CA 94303

Customer Service: 800-497-6138
www.teachtci.com

ISBN 1-58371-301-8

6 7 8 9 10 11 12 13 14   14 13 12 11 10 09 08

Program Directors

Bert Bower

Jim Lobdell

Program Author

Vicki LaBoskey, Professor of Education,
Mills College, Oakland, California
Ph.D., Curriculum and Teacher Education,
Stanford University, Stanford, California

Student Edition Authors

Laura M. Alavosus

John Bergez

Senior Curriculum Developer

Kelly Shafsky

Reading Specialist

Barbara Schubert, Reading Specialist,
Saint Mary's College, Moraga, California
Ph.D., Education, University of California,
Santa Barbara, California

Teacher Consultants

Judy Brodigan, Elementary Social Studies
Supervisor, Lewisville Independent
School District, Texas

Ann Dawson, Educational Consultant,
Intermediate Curriculum Specialist
Gahanna, Ohio

Candetta Holdren, Elementary Teacher,
Linlee Elementary, Lexington, Kentucky

Elizabeth McKenna, Elementary Teacher,
St. Thomas Aquinas Catholic School,
Diocese of Orlando, Florida

Lisa West, Instructional Specialist, Language Arts/
Social Studies, Landis Elementary School,
Houston, Texas

Beth Yankee, Elementary Teacher,
The Woodward School for Technology
and Research, Kalamazoo, Michigan

Internet and Literature Consultant

Debra Elsen, Elementary Teacher,
Manchester Elementary, Manchester, Maryland

Music Specialist

Beth Yankee, Elementary Teacher,
The Woodward School for Technology
and Research, Kalamazoo, Michigan

Geography Specialist

David Knipfer
Mapping Specialists, Ltd.
Madison, Wisconsin

Contents

Chapter 4
How Do People Become Part of Our Country?

Learn why and how immigrants come to the United States. Read about what life is like for an immigrant in the United States.

Chapter 5
What Makes Our Community Diverse?

Learn what the word culture means. Read about the foods, languages, holidays, and traditions that people share.

Chapter 6
How Do People Improve Their Communities?

Read about four famous people who helped their communities. Explore how one person can make a difference.

Chapter 7
How Are We Alike Around the World?

Discover what life is like in other countries. Read about six children your age. Learn how you are alike and different.

Where in the World Is Our Community?

Pretend you are an astronaut on the NASA space shuttle. If you looked at the planet Earth from space, what would you see? Clouds? Land? Water? What would you need to know to find your landing site on Earth?

In this chapter, you will learn about some geography terms, such as **hemispheres, continents, countries,** and **states**. Once you learn these terms, you can use maps to find any place on Earth.

Our Community Is
on Planet Earth

Earth looks big outside your window. (Remember that you are an astronaut in space.) How would you describe the shape of Earth? What else has this shape? A ball? Another word for this shape is **sphere**. If you cut a sphere in half, you get two hemispheres. **Hemisphere** means half of a sphere.

You can divide a sphere in half around the middle. Imagine a line running around the middle of Earth, like a belt that goes around your waist. We call that line the **equator**. It divides Earth into the Northern Hemisphere and the Southern Hemisphere.

Northern Hemisphere

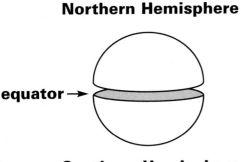

equator →

Southern Hemisphere

You can also divide a sphere in half from top to bottom. Imagine a line starting at the top of Earth and running around the bottom and back up to the top. We call that line the **prime meridian**. It divides Earth into the Western Hemisphere and the Eastern Hemisphere.

Western Hemisphere   **Eastern Hemisphere**

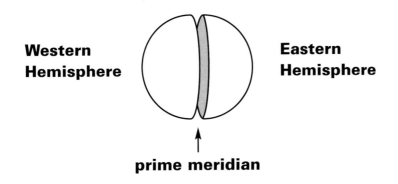

↑
prime meridian

What have you learned about Earth? Find the equator and the prime meridian on the maps. How many hemispheres do you see on these maps?

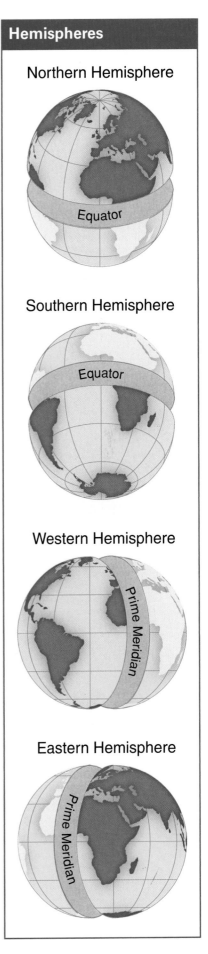

Hemispheres

Northern Hemisphere

Equator

Southern Hemisphere

Equator

Western Hemisphere

Prime Meridian

Eastern Hemisphere

Prime Meridian

Our Community Is on a Continent

From space, you can see that most of Earth is covered with water. The largest bodies of water are called **oceans**. There are four oceans on Earth. They are called the Pacific Ocean, the Atlantic Ocean, the Indian Ocean, and the Arctic Ocean. Look at the map to find the four oceans.

The four oceans wrap around large bodies of land. These areas of land are called **continents**. There are seven continents on Earth. They are called Africa, Asia, Antarctica, Australia, Europe, North America, and South America.

Oceans and Continents

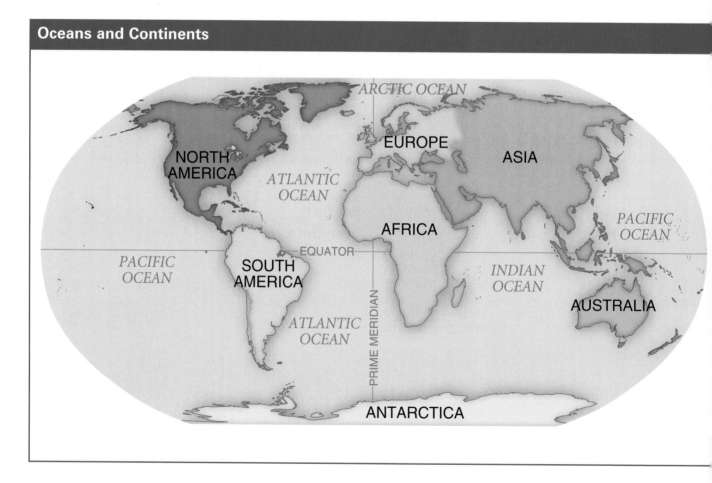

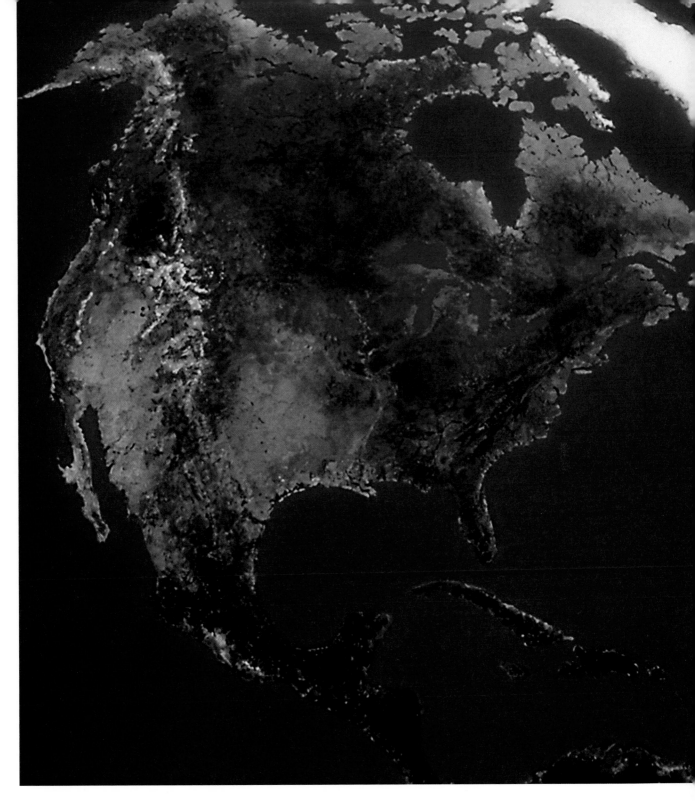

Asia is the largest continent. Australia is the smallest. Look at the map to find each of the seven continents.

On which continent do you live? Do you live near an ocean?

Our Community Is in a Country

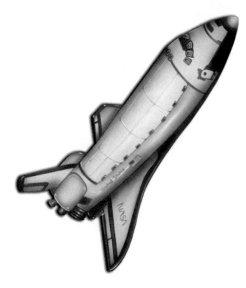

Now you are heading the space shuttle for your continent. What part of the continent do you need to find?

Most continents are made up of many **countries**. Each country has its own government. Some countries, such as Canada and the United States, are very large. Other countries, such as Cuba and El Salvador, are much smaller.

How can we tell where one country ends and another begins? On a map, we see lines drawn around each country. These lines show a country's borders. Mountains, rivers, and oceans can be borders. Other countries have to decide where to put their borders. How many countries can you find on the map below?

Each country has its own government. Most people in a country speak the same language. They often celebrate the same holidays. Find your country on the map below.

Countries

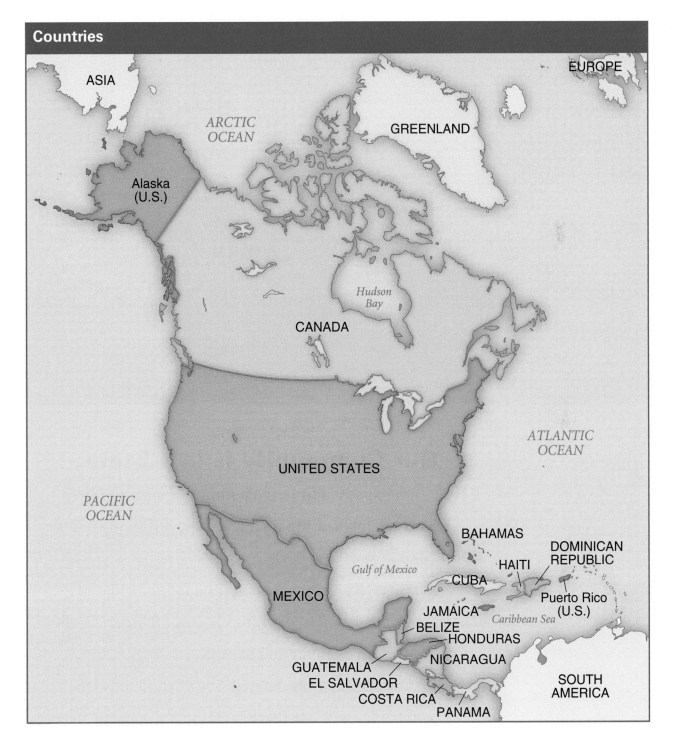

9

Our Community Is in a State

The space shuttle is zooming in on the United States. This is a big country. How will you find the landing spot?

Most large countries are divided into lots of smaller parts. In the United States of America, these smaller parts are called **states.**

The states of the United States show how the country grew. First there were only 13 states. They were on the eastern coast of the country. Then people started moving west. They made more states. Now there are 50 states in the United States of America.

The map shows that you're headed for the southeastern region of the United States. How many states are on this map?

Finding Communities in a State

Somewhere in the state on this map is a community with your landing spot. NASA will tell you how to find it. But first you need to learn how to find your way around in a state.

States are made up of many communities. Communities are places where people live, work, and play. Some communities have lots of buildings and people. We call them **cities**. New York and Los Angeles are cities. Other communities are smaller. We call them **towns**. Do you live in a town or a city?

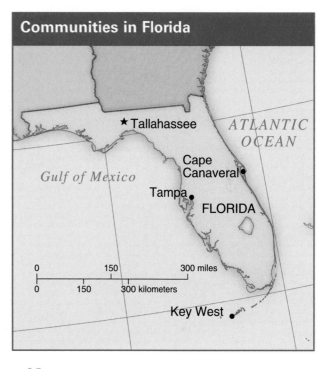

Communities in Florida

Wrap-Up

Congratulations. Your space shuttle flight back to Earth was a success. Now you know how to find a community anywhere in the world. Can you find where *you* live?

11

Where in the United States Is Our Community?

Your community is the place where you live. What is the name of the town or city where you live? Can you find your town or city on a map of the United States?

We use maps when we travel from one place to another. Maps show directions. North, south, east, and west are the **cardinal directions**.

In this chapter, you will find your community on a map of the United States. You'll read about some famous places and find them on a map, too.

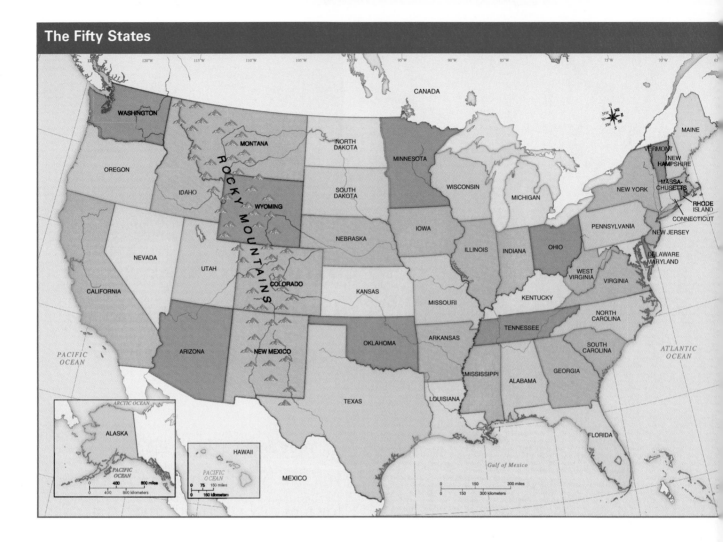

The Fifty States

When you write your address, you write the name of your street, the name of your city, and the name of the state where you live.

There are 50 states in the United States. Each state has lots of communities in it.

Which state do you live in?

14

The Statue of Liberty

Look at this picture. It shows a very big statue. This famous statue welcomes people to the United States. It stands for freedom. We call it the Statue of Liberty.

Many people visit the Statue of Liberty every year. It is on a small island in the city of New York. New York City is in the state of New York. New York is near the Atlantic Ocean.

Do you live near New York City?

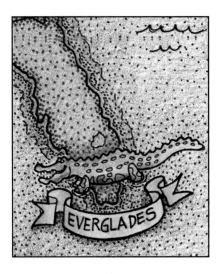

The Everglades

Have you ever seen an alligator? Would you like to meet a crocodile? You can in a famous place called the Everglades.

Lots of birds and reptiles live in the Everglades. It is very warm and wet there. People visit the Everglades to fish and camp and see wildlife.

The Everglades are in the state of Florida. Florida is east of the Gulf of Mexico.

Do you live north or south of the Everglades?

Mount Rushmore

Look at the faces carved into this mountain. Do you know who they are?

Mount Rushmore shows the faces of four U.S. presidents. The faces are 60 feet high. It took 14 years to carve them.

Mount Rushmore is in the state of South Dakota. South Dakota is west of the Mississippi River. It is east of the Rocky Mountains.

Do you live east or west of the Rocky Mountains?

The Grand Canyon

Why do you think we call this place the Grand Canyon? Grand means large. The Grand Canyon is 277 miles long and 1 mile down from its top to its bottom.

Visitors to the Grand Canyon can look down into it from the North and South Rims. Many people hike or ride mules down to the bottom. A river runs along the bottom of the canyon.

The Grand Canyon is in the state of Arizona. Arizona is east of the Pacific Ocean. It is west of the Mississippi River.

Do you live near a river?

The Golden Gate Bridge

The Golden Gate Bridge crosses the entrance to San Francisco Bay. Its name comes from the gold rush days. Men on their way to the goldfields called the bay the Golden Gate.

The Golden Gate Bridge opened in 1937. It was the tallest structure west of New York City.

The city of San Francisco is at the south end of the Golden Gate Bridge. People cross the bridge to get to other parts of the state of California.

Do you live near a famous bridge?

Wrap-Up

There are lots of fun places in the United States. Think about the places and states you learned about in this chapter. Which would you like to visit?

What Is the Geography of Our Community?

What do you think of when you hear the word **geography**? You might think about maps and globes. You might think about mountains and oceans.

In the last chapter, you learned geography skills to help you find places on a map. Geography can also tell us what it's like to live in those places.

In this chapter, you'll learn more about geography. You'll read about three different places in the United States.

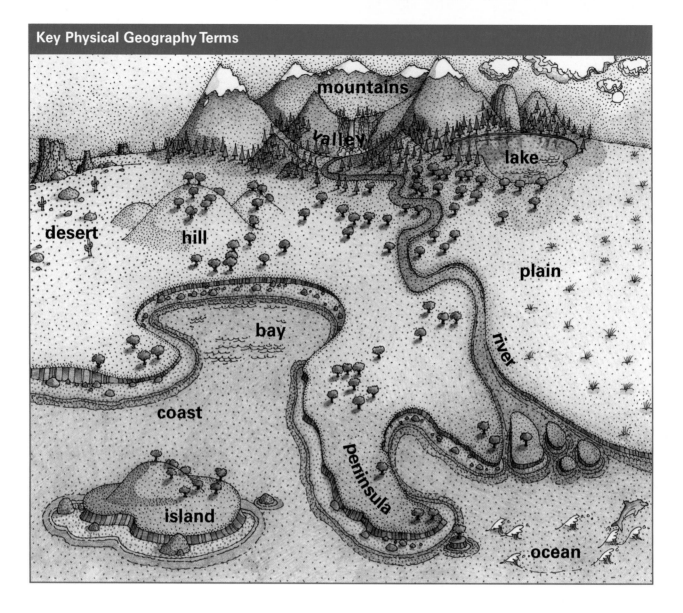

What Is Geography?

Geography is more than just maps. It's also about the weather and what the land looks like nearby. People use things around them in nature, like trees and water. These things are part of geography, too.

Look out a window. What do you see? Tall mountains or flat plains? A large lake or a river? These are all parts of the **physical geography** of a community. What are some of the features of the physical geography where you live?

Climate describes the weather in a place. Some places are warm and sunny. Other places can be cold and snowy. It rains a lot in some communities. In others, it almost never rains. In most places, the climate is different in the summer and winter. What is the climate like where you live?

People use lots of things from nature in their daily lives. These things are called **natural resources**. Water, land, fish, and trees are natural resources. People use wood from trees to build houses. They use land and water to grow food. What are the natural resources in your community?

The Geography of Roseburg, Oregon

The city of Roseburg, Oregon, is in the northwest region of the United States. Roseburg is about 70 miles east of the Pacific Ocean. What do you know about the geography of the Pacific Northwest?

Roseburg is in a valley of the Cascade Mountains. Tall trees cover the mountains. There are lots of rivers around Roseburg. A big river runs through the town. Mountains, trees, and rivers are all part of the physical geography of Roseburg.

The climate in Roseburg is gentle and mild. Winters are cool and rainy. Summers are warm and

dry. It never gets very cold or very hot. People like
to fish and go boating in the rivers around Roseburg.

Roseburg's climate also helps plants and trees
grow. Forests are the most important natural
resource in Roseburg.
People work in lumber
mills. They cut down
trees and send lumber to
other places. Lumber
mills have been in
Roseburg for many
years. Some people make
sure that more trees are
planted to replace those
cut down. Do you think
this is a good idea?

The Geography of Las Cruces, New Mexico

The city of Las Cruces, New Mexico, is in the southwest region of the United States. Las Cruces is about 50 miles north of the country of Mexico. What do you know about the geography of the Southwest?

The physical geography of Las Cruces has three important features. Las Cruces is in the middle of a desert. There are also mountains nearby. The city was built next to a big river, called the Rio Grande. Have you ever heard of the Rio Grande?

Las Cruces has a desert climate. The weather is hot and dry most of the time. In the summer, it grows very hot. Temperatures often climb over 100 degrees. It does not rain much in Las Cruces.

The desert has very little water. But water is the most important natural resource in Las Cruces. Are you surprised? People need water for drinking, washing, and watering plants. The people who live in Las Cruces use their water wisely. They are careful not to waste it. Would you like to visit this city in the desert?

The Geography of Gloucester, Massachusetts

The city of Gloucester (glaw-ster), Massachusetts, is in the northeast region of the United States. It is part of New England. What do you know about the geography of the Northeast?

The most important part of the physical geography of Gloucester is the ocean. Gloucester has ocean water on three sides. The shore is rocky with a few sandy beaches. Which ocean is near Gloucester? Look at the map to find out.

The climate changes from season to season in

Gloucester. Summers are warm and sunny. Winters are cold and snowy. Spring and fall are cool and rainy. The weather also changes from day to day. People there will tell you, "If you don't like the weather today, wait 'til tomorrow!"

Weather and the ocean mean a lot to the people of Gloucester. Fish and seafood are the most important natural resources. People work on fishing boats. They spend days at sea. When they return, they sell their catches of fish. Many people dig clams or trap lobsters to eat or to sell. Would you like to visit this New England seaport?

Wrap-Up

People decide to visit or live in a place for lots of reasons. They might like the climate. They might think the views are beautiful. They might get a job working with the natural resources. All of these things are part of the geography of a place. What is important to you when you go to new places?

How Do People Become Part of Our Country?

Lots of different people live in the United States. But how did we all get here? Some people have lived here for thousands of years. But most arrived fewer than 200 years ago.

Some people chose to come to America. Other people were forced to come.

When people choose to leave one country and live in another country, they are called **immigrants**. In this chapter, you will learn why and how immigrants come to the United States.

Why Immigrants Come to the United States

Immigrants come to the United States for many reasons. Sometimes people need to get away from problems where they live. Problems might be things like war or unfair laws. Another problem is too many people. When there are too many people, there may not be enough jobs or food for everyone.

Once there wasn't enough food in the country of Ireland. Potato plants stopped growing. People didn't have enough to eat. Many Irish people went to America when this happened.

People move for other reasons, too. Sometimes they want a better life. They may see a chance to do that in another country.

Our country grew quickly about 200 years ago. People came from all over the world. Some came from Europe to buy land in America. Others came when gold was discovered out west. They hoped to get rich. Most didn't make fortunes, but they stayed in America anyway.

How do you think other immigrants get to the United States?

How Immigrants Get to the United States

Getting to America is not easy. It costs a lot to travel to the United States. Sometimes a whole family will save money. Then just one person will use that money to get to America.

Today, immigrants must also get permission to come to the United States. This means filling out lots of papers. It means standing in long lines to turn in the papers. It also means waiting. Sometimes it takes years to get permission.

The trip to the United States can be hard. In the past, some immigrants from China spent weeks on crowded ships. Others from Mexico walked hundreds of miles. Many immigrants risk their lives getting to the United States.

Arriving in America wasn't easy, either. Many immigrants arrived at a place called Ellis Island in New York. At Ellis Island, doctors examined them. They had to answer questions. Most immigrants didn't speak English. Often, they didn't understand the tests. Sometimes they were sent back home if they didn't pass the tests. Immigrants felt lucky if they were able to stay in America.

What do you think life is like for immigrants in the United States?

Life for Immigrants in the United States

Immigrants often find that life in America can be hard. Sometimes people **discriminate** against immigrants. To discriminate means to treat unfairly. Immigrants might have to take jobs that no one else wants. These jobs can be dangerous. They might not pay much money. Families have to work hard to make enough money for the things they need.

Immigrants also find good things about life in the United States. They might have more freedom than before. They can practice their religions here. They have more choices in America. They might be able to make more money than before.

Some immigrants even become famous or important people in the United States. Carlos Santana is an immigrant from Mexico. He became a famous musician in America. Madeleine Albright is an immigrant from a country in Europe. She became an important leader in the United States.

Wrap-Up

Immigrants from all over the world have come to the United States. It takes hard work to get here. In America, immigrants hope to make a better life.

What Makes Our Community Diverse?

In the last chapter, you learned how and why people have come to the United States. The United States is a diverse nation. **Diverse** means made up of different groups of people.

A group of people often have things in common. They may speak the same language or eat the same kinds of foods. They may celebrate the same holidays and wear similar clothes. They may play the same games and sports. These things are part of a group's culture. A **culture** is a way of life shared by a group of people.

Our Community Shares Different Foods

Food is an important part of any culture. When people move to a new place, they often make and eat the same foods they are used to. Their neighbors may eat different kinds of foods. In communities around the United States, different cultures often share foods with each other.

Europeans have brought many foods to our communities. You have probably eaten pasta from the Italian culture, waffles from the culture of Germany, and bagels from the Jewish culture. Have you ever tasted Russian borscht (a cold soup made from beets) or a Greek gyro (roasted lamb in a pocket of pita bread)?

Asian Americans also have brought their cultures' foods to the United States. Have you eaten Japanese sushi? Or Chinese chow mein? What about pho (a hearty soup of noodles and meat) from Vietnam? Or tandoori chicken (a spicy chicken dish) from India?

Many Americans like to eat foods shared by Latino cultures. Tacos and tamales are popular Mexican American foods. Gallo pinto is a dish of fried rice and black beans from Costa Rica.

African Americans share such foods as hush puppies (fried cornmeal) and hoppin' john (a stew of pork, rice, and black-eyed peas).

What are some of the foods that people eat in your community? What cultures do you think first ate these foods?

Our Community Shares Different Languages

Most people in the United States speak English. Many people also use other languages in their homes and communities.

Most people whose families came from Mexico and Central or South America belong to Latino cultures. They might speak Spanish in their homes and communities. Anyone who speaks English also knows some words in Spanish. That's because words like patio and mosquito were borrowed from Spanish words. The names of places like Florida and San Francisco also came from Spanish names.

In some communities, people speak Native American languages. Native Americans have lived in what is now the United States for thousands of years.

There are many Native American languages, including Cherokee and Navajo. Many words and names we use in English—such as skunk, tomato, and Kentucky—are borrowed from Native American languages.

The English language comes from Europe. In some communities around the United States, people speak other European languages, such as French, German, Greek, and Swedish. Kindergarten, poodle, and atlas are words in English that were brought to this country by European Americans.

What are some of the languages that people use in your community? What languages do you use at home?

Our Community Shares Holidays

People celebrate many different holidays in communities around the United States. Holidays are times when we remember important people or events. They are special days when we celebrate or have a party. Each culture remembers its own special days and people.

People from Europe have brought many holidays to the United States. Halloween, St. Patrick's Day, and Valentine's Day are all holidays that have been celebrated for hundreds of years in European cultures.

During the month of December, three different cultures celebrate three different holidays in the

United States. African American families celebrate the holiday of Kwanzaa. Jewish families celebrate the holiday of Hanukkah. Many Christian cultures share the holiday of Christmas.

The fifth of May is an important day to different cultures in the United States. It is Children's Day to Japanese Americans. It is Cinco de Mayo to Mexican Americans. Cinco de Mayo honors a famous battle in Mexican history.

Different cultures celebrate the new year in different ways. Most people celebrate the New Year on the first day of January. The Chinese culture, however, celebrates their New Year on a different date each year. Their celebration lasts for 15 days.

What are some of the holidays celebrated in your community? What holidays do you share with your family and friends?

Our Community Shares Cultural Traditions

Each culture has its own **traditions**. Traditions are things that people do together year after year. Traditions might involve games, sports, clothing, and the arts.

Many popular sports in America are traditions of different cultures. The sports of soccer, golf, ice-skating, and skiing were brought to America by cultures from Europe. Surfing is a sport first shared by the Polynesian culture of the Hawaiian Islands.

Cultures also share their traditions in the arts. American musical traditions of jazz, gospel, and rock and roll began with contributions by African American artists. Salsa and tango music and dance have roots with Latino cultures. Asian Americans

share traditions in puppetry and drama.

Almost every culture has a traditional dance to share. Do you know how to clog? Or belly dance? Clogging is an American tradition started by European Americans from Ireland, Scotland, and the Netherlands. Belly dancing is a tradition of Middle Eastern cultures.

What are some traditions that cultures share in your community? What are some favorite traditions in your family?

Wrap-Up

The American culture has its own traditions, too. Americans play baseball and football. We celebrate Thanksgiving. We eat foods like hot dogs and apple pie. These are all part of our American culture. Can you think of other examples?

47

How Do People Improve Their Communities?

Communities grow and change all the time. As their communities grow, people need to solve problems. They try to make their town or city a better place to live. Just one person can make a big difference.

Read on to learn about four people who helped others. They each solved a problem in their community. Do you know anyone who has helped make a community a better place to live?

César Chávez Helped Make Life Better for Farmworkers

César Chávez was born in 1927 near Yuma, Arizona. When he was 11 years old, his family moved to California. A few years later, César started working as a **farmworker**. He moved from farm to farm picking crops. He often worked 12 hours a day or more.

César wanted to help farmworkers have better lives. So, in 1962, he started a group to help them.

His group was called the United Farm Workers, or UFW for short.

One of the communities that the UFW helped was Delano, California. In Delano, farmworkers labored long hours for very little pay. Many workers had serious accidents because of unsafe tools and machines. César helped these workers join together to ask for better pay and safer working conditions.

At first, the farm owners refused to listen to César and the workers. So, César told all the workers to stop

working. This is called a **strike**. The workers hoped
their strike would make the farm owners pay
attention to them. Then César convinced people to
stop buying what the farms sold. This is called a
boycott. After many years, the farm owners finally
gave in. They agreed to pay the farmworkers more
and to improve safety.

César Chávez made a difference in the community
of Delano. He helped make Delano a better place for
farmworkers. César continued to help farmworkers
in communities all across the country.

Ruby Bridges Helped Make Life Better for African Americans

In 1960, Ruby Bridges was six years old. She lived in New Orleans, Louisiana, and was ready to

start first grade. Ruby was about to make history.

She would be the first African American student to go to a white school. Ruby was proud to be part of this important event.

On her first day, Ruby walked to school with two special policemen by her side. The president of the United States had sent them to protect her. Angry crowds of people outside the school yelled and threw things at her. They said, "Blacks don't belong in our schools!" Ruby thought some of them hated her enough to hurt her.

Inside the school,

Ruby discovered she was the only student there. All the other kids had stayed home. For months, Ruby was the only student in class. After a while, people realized that Ruby wasn't going to go away. Two white children came to school with her one day. Then more and more students returned to school.

Ruby Bridges made a difference in her community. She finished first grade at Frantz Elementary School. She also graduated from high school. Later, her four sons went to school in New Orleans with other black and white children. They didn't have to walk through crowds of angry people. Now children of all races in the United States have the right to go to good schools.

Lois Marie Gibbs Helped Make Her Community Safer

In 1979, Lois Gibbs was 27 years old. She lived in Niagara Falls, New York. Lois had two children, Michael and Melissa. They were both very sick. Lois wanted to know why.

There was an old **canal,** or waterway, near Michael's school. It was called Love Canal.

Businesses had been dumping dangerous chemicals into it for years. The canal flowed underneath the school playground. Lois thought the dirty canal was making her children sick.

Lois didn't know what to do. No one believed her fears about Love Canal. Lois asked her neighbors about their health. It turned out that more than half of the kids in the area were sick, too. Some scientists agreed that the canal could be the problem. Lois decided to do something about it.

Lois Gibbs got all her neighbors together. They knew they needed help. They decided

to tell everyone they could about their problem.

They carried signs and followed the governor of their state around. People saw them on television.

Finally, the governor visited Love Canal. He agreed to help families move to a safer place. Later, President Jimmy Carter helped more families move.

Lois Gibbs helped the people in her community. She made a difference in many people's lives. Today, Lois Gibbs helps people all over the country work together to make their communities safer.

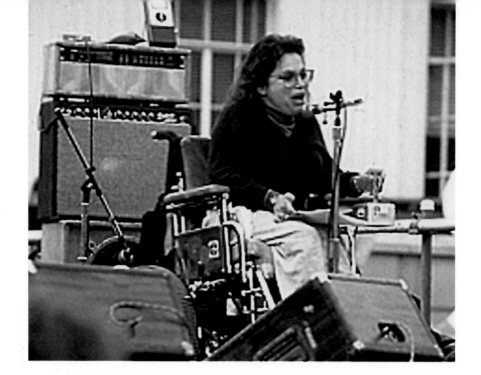

Judy Heumann Helped Make Life Better for Disabled People

Judy Heumann was born in 1947. She was a healthy baby. Then, she got sick with a disease called polio. She was only a year and a half old. The disease hurt her legs. She would never be able to walk. Judy grew up using a wheelchair to get around.

Judy lived in Brooklyn, New York. On Judy's first day of first grade, her mother brought her to school. But the principal wouldn't let Judy in because she was in a wheelchair. The school sent a teacher to Judy's house twice a week instead.

Finally, in the middle of fourth grade, the city agreed to let Judy go to school. She went to a special classroom for disabled students. **Disabled** means needing help to do things like walk or talk.

At school, Judy met other disabled people and

learned that others felt the way she did. Her legs didn't work right, but her brain was just fine. She wanted to learn as much as every other student in the school.

Later, Judy went to college to be a teacher. When she graduated, New York City wouldn't let her teach because she was in a wheelchair. She sued the city and won. Judy then taught elementary school for three years.

Later Judy decided to help other disabled people. She formed a group called Disabled in Action. This group helps protect disabled people from being treated unfairly. Judy Heumann's work has helped many disabled people live better lives.

Wrap-Up

These people all made a difference in their communities. They helped improve other people's lives. How could you make a difference in your community?

How Are We Alike Around the World?

You probably get up at the same time each morning. You and your friends probably do similar things every day. What do children in other parts of the world do each day?

Some things are the same no matter where we live. Everyone wakes up in the morning. Children go to school. People have work to do.

In this chapter, you will read about the lives of six children. Each child lives in a different country. As you read, think about how each child's day is like yours.

8

How Does Our Economy Work?

Have you ever been to a farmers **market**? Farmers markets are places where farmers bring their crops to sell.

A farmers market is only one kind of market. A market is any place where buyers and sellers come together.

Much of our community's **economy** involves buying and selling. How do sellers decide what price to charge for their goods? Why do some goods cost more than others? In this chapter, you will explore these questions.

We Buy and Sell Things

Imagine that you're a farmer. It's early summer. You have ripe green beans to sell.

As a farmer, you are a seller. What price will you charge for your beans? You want to get as much money as you can. But you don't want to charge too much. Customers might not want to pay your price. They might go to another farmer who is selling green beans at a lower price.

Now imagine that you're a customer at the farmers market. You are now a buyer. You want to buy as many green beans as you can for your money. You also want the best green beans for the lowest price. You might shop around to see what different farmers want for their green beans.

As this example shows, markets bring together people who have different goals. Sellers want prices to be as high as possible. Buyers want prices to be as low as possible. Sellers are all trying to sell to the same customers. But customers have choices.

So, how do prices get set in a market? A big part of the answer is something called **supply** and **demand**.

Prices Change When Supply Is High and Demand Is Low

All of the oranges for sale at a farmers market make up the supply of oranges at the market. Supply is the total amount of a product for sale. The amount of oranges that customers want to buy is called the demand for oranges. The demand for a product is the total amount that customers will buy at a certain price.

The supply and demand of a product can affect the price. Let's look at what happens when supply is high and demand is low.

Imagine that it's December. Many farmers have brought lots of ripe oranges to market. The supply of oranges is high.

But customers bought lots of oranges last month. They want to buy peaches this week. Demand for oranges is low.

Now the farmers have a problem. They have more oranges than customers want to buy. What do the farmers do? One thing they can do is lower their prices. If they make their prices low enough, customers might decide to buy some oranges after all.

In fact, the farmers may compete with each other by making their prices lower and lower to attract buyers. So, when supply is high and demand is low, prices go down.

Tas... BANANAS 25¢/lb.

MORE CHERRIES LATER!

...us APPLES 60¢/l

Bing CHERRIES 2 o

Juicy 4

$3⁵⁰ per lb.

ABOUT TOWN Fresh Mayer LEMONS 5/$1

Prices Change When Demand Is High and Supply Is Low

Can you guess what happens to prices when demand is high and supply is low? Imagine that it is late July. The season for cherries is almost over. Few farmers have ripe cherries to sell. The supply of cherries is low.

But many customers at the market want to buy cherries. The demand for cherries is high.

Now the customers have a problem. The demand for cherries is greater than the supply. What do the customers do? Customers can compete with each other to get the cherries. They do this by being willing to pay more for the cherries than other customers. The farmers know this, so they raise their prices. They know that buyers will pay more for something when there is less of it.

So, when demand is high and supply is low, prices go up.

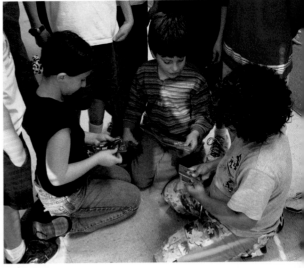

Have you ever collected trading cards? If so, you may have experienced supply and demand. Suppose you have a card that everyone else has. Your friends probably won't give you much for it. The supply of that card is high, and the demand is low. So, the price people will pay for the card is low.

What happens if you have a rare trading card? Your friends might trade two or three cards for it. That's because the supply of that card is low, while demand is high. Now the price of the card is high.

Changes in Supply or Demand Cause Changes in Price

You've seen that prices change when supply and demand change. But what makes supply and demand change?

Many things can affect the supply of a product. Suppose farmers in California have grown a huge crop of watermelons. There are more watermelons than anyone has seen in 25 years. The supply of watermelons goes way up. Now farmers will have to lower their prices in order to sell all their melons.

They know that customers will buy more watermelons at lower prices.

Now suppose that there's a winter freeze in Florida. This weather spoils half of the year's crop of oranges. The supply of oranges is now small. There aren't enough oranges for everyone who wants them. Farmers can raise their prices now. They know that customers will pay more for the oranges.

80

Many things can make demand go up and down, too. Suppose that millions of basketball fans see a famous player drinking apple juice on television. The fans may decide that drinking apple juice is a good way to increase their energy. More people want to buy apple juice now. The demand for apple juice goes up, and so does the price.

Here's another example. It's the day after Halloween. All across the country, pumpkin farms still have pumpkins to sell. The week before Halloween, demand for pumpkins was high. Prices went up. Now that Halloween is over, demand is low. So, pumpkin farms lower their prices.

Wrap-Up

The idea of supply and demand helps explain how markets work. Together, supply and demand change the prices that sellers charge for their goods.

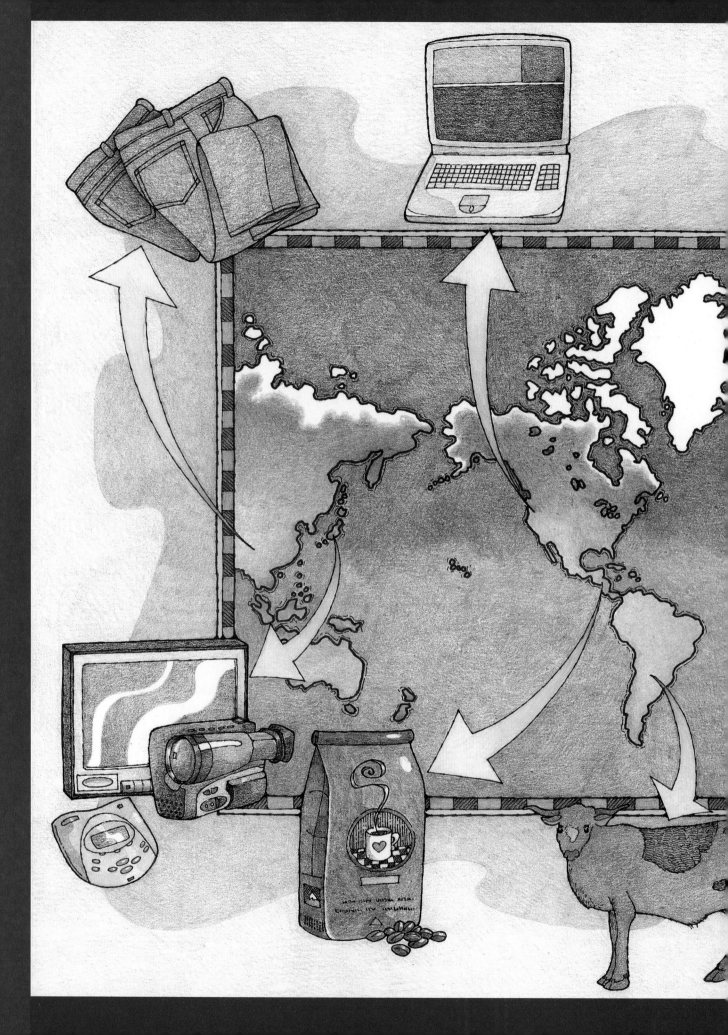

9

How Does Global Trade Affect Our Community?

It takes the whole world to get Jen to school in the morning.

Jen's clock radio wakes her up. The radio was made in Japan. Then Jen puts on her jeans and her favorite T-shirt. They were made in China. Jen's athletic shoes were made in Thailand.

For breakfast, Jen eats a banana that came from Ecuador. Then she rides to school in a car that was made in Germany. The gas in the car comes from oil found in Saudi Arabia.

You, too, use things each day that come from all over the world. In this chapter, you will learn how your community gets these things.

Our Country Trades What We Have for What We Need

Have you ever traded things with your friends? Maybe you traded an apple for a banana at lunch. Or maybe you traded a coloring book for a ball and jacks.

Trades work when people have things that other people want. The same is true of countries. For example, Ecuador grows lots of bananas. The United States grows few bananas. So, the United States buys bananas from Ecuador.

What does Ecuador need? Farmers in Ecuador need tractors. The United States has many factories that make tractors. So, Ecuador buys tractors from the United States.

Ecuador sells bananas to the United States. The United States sells tractors to Ecuador. You could say that Ecuador trades its bananas for tractors. In the same way, the United States trades its tractors for bananas.

These kinds of trades go on all over the world. Together, they are called **global trade**. Today, global trade is bigger than ever before. That's because people have figured out better ways to move and store goods.

Some Natural Resources Come from Other Countries

Countries trade the natural resources they have for those they don't have. For example, banana trees grow best in hot, wet countries, such as Ecuador. Coffee plants grow best in mountains where it is warm and rains a lot. The countries of Guatemala and Kenya grow a lot of coffee.

Wheat grows better in parts of the United States than in other countries. So, the United States sells lots of wheat to other countries. It buys most of its

An oil rig.

coffee and bananas from other countries.

The United States has its own oil, gold, and copper. But the United States doesn't have enough of these resources to meet its needs. So it trades other goods to countries that have these resources to sell. For instance, the Middle Eastern country of Saudi Arabia is very rich in oil. South Africa is famous for its gold and diamond mines. And the South American country of Chile sells more copper than any other country in the world.

Some Products Come from Other Countries

Countries also trade things that they make, or **manufacture**. Some examples are cars, televisions, computers, and shoes.

Some countries are famous for making high-quality goods. For example, many people like to buy watches made in Switzerland. Companies in Japan make reliable televisions and radios. German factories make some of the world's best cars. Some companies in the United States are very good at making computers.

Other countries want these goods because of their quality. So, they trade their own products to get them.

Some countries can make goods for less money than other countries. For example, many Asian countries can make clothes at a low cost. Companies in Asia pay their workers less money than companies in other countries. This lowers the price of the clothes they make.

Other countries buy goods because of their low price. Once again, they will trade their own products to get them. That is one reason your jeans, T-shirts, and athletic shoes may come from countries in Asia.

Pros and Cons of Global Trade

There are good things **(pros)** and bad things **(cons)** about global trade.

What are some of the pros? Global trade allows people to buy things from all over the world. It allows people to enjoy quality goods. It also allows people to pay less for some goods. Without global trade, Jen might not have bananas for breakfast. Jen's dad might not have a nice car. And Jen's athletic shoes might cost a lot more if they were made in the United States.

What are some of the cons? Global trade allows companies to move to countries where the pay is low. It keeps the pay low for workers in poorer countries. Suppose a shoe company moves its factories from the

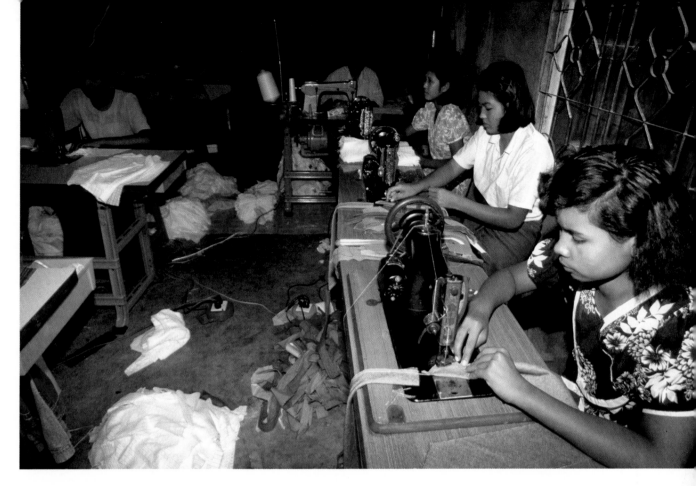

United States to Thailand. The workers in the United States lose their jobs. The shoe company might pay very little to its workers in Thailand. If the workers complain, the company can move somewhere else.

Also, global trade means that people don't always have to buy things made locally. So, companies in their own countries could lose business. Jen's father didn't buy an American car. Instead, he bought a car from Germany. Japanese computer makers lose business if people in Japan buy American computers.

Wrap-Up

Global trade connects the countries of the world. It brings many good things to people. It can also create problems for people around the world.

10

What Are the Public Services in Our Community?

Public services make our communities better places to live. Services are things that other people do for you. Public means the services are for everyone.

Usually, you have to pay for services. Public services are different. They are services that everyone in a community needs. So, most towns and cities provide them free or at low cost to their citizens.

What kinds of services are public services? You'll find out in this chapter.

Fire Fighting

Fire fighting is an important service. Firefighters risk their lives to save people and homes from fires.

Firefighters also try to keep fires from happening. They teach people what to do to prevent fires. They make sure businesses obey fire safety laws.

Firefighters help people in other ways, too. They help people who are hurt in accidents. They rescue people and animals. They help people in floods, hurricanes, and earthquakes.

Firefighters everywhere wear the same kind of clothing. They need to protect themselves from the heat and flames of a fire. They wear thick jackets, heavy gloves, and waterproof pants and boots.

Long ago, people had to fight their own fires. When a fire broke out, everyone in town rushed to the scene. They formed a line and passed buckets of water to help put out the fire.

Today, fire fighting is a public service in most places. Some firefighters are **volunteers**. They are not paid for their services. All firefighters today are well trained. Is fire fighting a public service in your community?

Public Transportation

How do people get from place to place where you live? Do they ride bicycles or walk? Do they drive cars? Do they take buses or trains? Most communities have some kind of public transportation.

Public buses take people from one part of a city to another. Some travel between cities. Large cities also have **subways**. Subways are trains that run under the ground. Many other cities have **streetcars**. Streetcars are small trains that use city streets. Some public trains run between cities and their suburbs.

COMMUNITY BIKE PARK

PLEASE LEAVE AND COLLECT YOUR COMMUNITY BIKES FROM THIS SITE

The Cambridge City Community Bike Scheme provides free bikes for use by the Community as part of the "Safer Cambridge Initiative". Users of the scheme should pick up bikes from the Bike Parks around the city and leave them at a Bike Park near to their destination for someone else to use. Community Bikes are painted bright green, and carry the above logo.

TERMS AND CONDITIONS OF USE

PLEASE CHECK THAT THE BIKE IS ROADWORTHY BEFORE USE.
If you detect a fault, please report it by telephoning 416577.

Bikes are for Community use. Do not lock Community Bikes.

If a bike is to be used after dark, please attach lights.

Bikes are for use within the City of Cambridge only.

Persons caught damaging or stealing Community Bikes will be prosecuted. If you see a bike being damaged or stolen, please telephone 416577.

Please ride and park bikes safely, and with consideration for pedestrians and other road users.

DISCLAIMER
THE CAMBRIDGE COMMUNITY BIKE SCHEME ACCEPTS NO RESPONSIBILITY FOR ANY LOSS, DAMAGE, OR PERSONAL INJURY INCURRED BY PERSONS USING COMMUNITY BIKES.

ANOTHER SAFER CITY INITIATIVE

In most places, you pay a **fare** to use public transportation. But the fare is usually low enough that almost everyone can afford it.

Public transportation helps people get around. It also helps create less traffic and less pollution. When people all drive their own cars, streets and highways get crowded. All those cars pollute the air.

In some cities, you can borrow a bicycle for free. People like public bicycles. They don't cause any pollution at all!

Do you think people would use public bicycles where you live?

Child Care

In many families, parents work at jobs all day. How do they make sure their children are safe while they are at work? Most of these families use child care services.

Child care services are usually centers where parents can leave their children during the day. At child care centers, children play with each other. They often do art projects and sing songs. They have snacks, listen to stories, and take naps. Child care workers are trained to take care of children's needs.

Child care is important, but it is not free for most people in the United States. Families have to pay for child care. It can be very expensive. Some people have to pay almost as much for child care as they

earn at their jobs. Then they don't have enough
money to pay for other things, such as food and
health care.

In some countries, child care is a public service.
For example, in Denmark and Vietnam child care is
free or costs very little. This makes it easier for
parents to work.

Do you think child care should be a public
service in your community?

Wrap-Up

Police, fire fighting, schools, and transportation
are public services in many communities. Health
care and child care are public services in some
places. What are the public services where you live?

MAYOR

CITY TO-DO LIST

CITY HALL

POLICE

11

Who Works at City Hall?

Does your community have a **city hall**? Maybe it's called a town hall. This building is where the government of your community has its offices.

The **government** includes the people who keep your community running smoothly. These people have many duties. Some of them make laws. Some of them keep important records. Others make sure that the city parks are clean or that the streetlights are working.

Do you know the people who work in your city hall? Do you know what they do? In this chapter, you will find out.

The Mayor and the City Council

The mayor is usually the head of the city council. There may be only 3 people on the council. Or there may be 12 or more.

The mayor and the members of the council want the community to be safe and clean. They also want to make the community a fun place to live. To do this, they make laws. **Laws** tell people what they can and cannot do. A city might have a law that says people must clean up after their pets. There might be a law about how fast people can drive on your street.

Hon.
Takeyoshi Nishio
Mayor, Nagoya, Japan

Hon.
Tom Bradley
Mayor of Los Angeles

The mayor and the city council have other people to help them. Police help make sure people obey the laws. Firefighters help keep the community safe. Other people help take care of parks and streets.

These people need money to do their jobs. The mayor and city council know how much money the town has to spend. They decide how much money to give to the schools and libraries. They decide how much to spend on roads and bridges.

The City Manager

Suppose a town decides to have a Kids' Day celebration. You might like to help. If so, you would talk to the city manager. The city manager would be in charge of planning this special day.

The mayor and the city council decide who will be the city manager. City managers make sure all the rest of the council's decisions happen.

City managers look for ways to make their communities better. They let the city council know what needs to be done.

City managers also make a plan for how to use the city's money. This plan is called a **budget**. The budget shows how much money each department can spend.

Not all communities have a city manager. Does yours?

The City Clerk

City clerks keep important records for the community. They keep lists of births and deaths. They give permits to people who want to add a room to their house or build a garage. They give people licenses to get married or to have a dog. They may also collect money for taxes.

The city clerk takes notes during city council meetings. Anyone in the town or city can read the city clerk's notes. This is one way that people can find out what their city council is doing.

City clerks have another very important job. They help run the city's elections. The city clerk tells voters where and when to vote. People can register to vote with their city clerk.

The Parks and Recreation Department

Do you know who takes care of the parks and playgrounds in your town or city? Most communities have a parks and recreation department. People who work in this department make sure parks are clean and safe.

They help the community in other ways, too. Sometimes playgrounds need a new slide. A park might need another bike path. The public pool might need repairing. The parks and recreation department does these things.

This department also plans fun things for people to do. Kids can join softball teams or take swimming lessons. Older people might play bingo or go on picnics.

The Public Library

Most towns and cities have a library. Large cities have a library in each neighborhood.

Libraries are quiet places. They have books, magazines, and newspapers. They have music and artwork, too. Many have computers for people to use.

People use libraries in different ways. Many people borrow books to read at home. Others like to sit and read newspapers from other parts of the world. Children listen to stories being read aloud.

Libraries are good for other things, too. They might have special events such as concerts and poetry readings. People can join reading groups at the public library. They can find out about services in their area.

The Fire Department

The fire department has two main jobs.

The first job is to help people in emergencies. Of course, firefighters put out fires. They also rescue people from dangerous places. They give medical care to people who are hurt.

The second job is to help people know what to do in an emergency. Have you had fire drills at school? The fire department helps you know what to do when there's a fire.

Suppose you want someone to tell your class what to do in an earthquake or a flood. Someone from the fire department would be a good choice.

The fire department prepares people for emergencies in other ways, too. They teach people how to prevent fires. They find out how fires start. They make sure buildings are safe.

The Police Department

The police help to keep people safe. They do this in two main ways.

First, the police try to catch people who break laws. For example, they give tickets to people who drive too fast. Do you see drivers speeding on your street? You could ask the police department to help stop them.

Second, the police try to stop crimes before they happen. That's why you see police walking or driving through neighborhoods. They are trying to make sure everyone obeys the laws.

The police also talk to people about how to prevent crimes. They tell students about what the police department does in their community. Do you know how to call the police department? When might you need to call them?

The Planning Department

Towns and cities are always changing and growing. People want to build houses and other buildings. But communities need parks and playgrounds, too.

The planning department helps decide which changes would be best. It divides a map of the town and city into areas called building zones. Some zones are for houses. Others are for businesses.

The planning department gives permission for new buildings. The idea for a new building must match the community's plan. For example, the building might be too tall for the area. It might cause too much traffic in a neighborhood. Or it might be just what people need in that spot.

The Public Works Department

The public works department helps keep a town or city working smoothly. It takes care of streets, bridges, stoplights, and water and sewer pipes. We call these things **public works**.

This department's main job is to keep public works in good shape. People who work for the public works department pave roads, repair cracks and holes, and fix other problems.

This department also builds new public works that a community needs as it grows. Does your town need more stoplights or a new city hall? The mayor and city council could vote to spend money on these projects. Then the public works department would do the work.

Wrap-Up

It takes a lot of people to run a town or city. The people who work at city hall have important jobs. The mayor and city council make most of the decisions. The city manager and city clerk help them. Other departments also help keep towns and cities running smoothly.

12

How Do We Have a Voice in Our Community?

Has your family ever made a decision about where to live or where to go for a vacation? Did anyone ask what you thought? If not, how did you feel? You may have felt upset or angry. We all like to have a voice in the decisions that affect us.

The same is true in your town or city. People want to have a voice in decisions that affect their lives.

In this chapter, you'll learn about ways you can have a voice in your community.

Going to Public Meetings

One way to have a voice in your community is to go to public meetings. Towns and cities have meetings to talk about important decisions. These decisions affect everyone who lives in the community.

Before making decisions, community leaders want to know what people think. They ask people to come to public meetings to share their thoughts and ideas.

Anyone can attend a public meeting. You can go just to listen. Or you can speak your opinion on a subject.

Only one person can speak at a time. Sometimes the leaders at a meeting will ask you a question. When you are finished, the next person gets to speak.

It can be hard to stand up in front of a group and talk. But if you are brave enough, a public meeting gives you a voice in your community. You can tell city leaders what you think. You can tell your neighbors, too. You might even change people's minds!

Attending Peaceful Demonstrations

Taking part in a peaceful demonstration is another way to make your voice heard. A **demonstration** is a gathering of people. **Peaceful** means to do something without hurting others.

Peaceful demonstrations let other people know about a problem in the community. People have peaceful demonstrations to show how they feel. They put words and pictures on posters and banners. They make speeches. They might march in a parade.

You can get a lot of people's attention with a peaceful demonstration. At a demonstration, you can share what you think and feel. You can also teach others about a problem you care about.

In the 1950s and 1960s, many people felt that changes needed to happen. They wanted all people to be treated the same. They held peaceful demonstrations to let others know how they felt.

Thousands of people marched in parades together. People all over the country saw the marches on television. They read about them in newspapers. Community leaders began to pay attention to them. The marches made everyone think more about equal treatment for all people.

Supporting a Candidate

A **candidate** is someone who runs for office. This means the person wants to do a job for the community. Helping a candidate is another way to have a voice in your community.

Helping, or supporting, candidates is a way to share your ideas. Candidates want to improve their community. To get elected, they tell voters about themselves and their ideas. People vote for the candidate who agrees with most of their ideas. In this way, you have a voice in decisions about your community.

How do candidates talk to voters? They give speeches. They talk to news reporters. They go to public places and shake hands with voters. Sometimes they even visit people's homes.

Candidates need lots of help to get elected. They can't talk to every single voter. So they need other people to tell their friends and neighbors about them and their ideas.

There are many ways to support a candidate. You can give money to help them. You can put signs in your yard or windows. You can make phone calls to ask people to vote for your candidate. You can talk to voters at shopping centers.

Voting

Voting is one of the most important ways to have a voice in your community. People vote in elections. Voters help to choose community leaders. They also vote on ideas for improving their town or city.

When the United States began, only a few people could vote. Back in the 1700s, you had to be a white man to vote. You also had to own land. Today, all men and women can vote.

There are a few rules about voting. You must be at least 18 years old. You must be a citizen of the United States. And you must sign up to vote.

On election day, people go to a polling place. They wait in line for their turn to vote. Then they go to a small booth. The booth is private so that no one else can see how they are voting.

People vote by marking a **ballot**. The ballot lists all the candidates and ideas to vote on. The candidates and ideas with the most votes win.

Most of the time, only leaders get to make decisions for the community. But, in an election, every voter helps choose one idea or candidate over another. In this way, voting gives people a strong voice in their community.

Wrap-Up

There are lots of ways to make your voice heard in your community. You can go to public meetings. You can attend demonstrations. You can support candidates for election. And, once you turn 18, you can vote.

127

13

Whose Planet Is It, Anyway?

We all want our planet to be a safe and healthful place. That means we need to protect Earth's air, water, and soil. We do this by fighting pollution. **Pollution** is anything that harms the air, water, or soil.

Pollution has many causes. Cars and factories send smoke into the air. Ships spill oil into the ocean. People sometimes dump dangerous chemicals onto the ground.

In this chapter, you will read about how three communities fight pollution.

Polluted Air

Tara Church was eight years old when she started to worry about air pollution. It all started with paper plates. Tara was a Brownie in the Girl Scouts. She and her Brownie friends were planning to take paper plates on a camping trip.

"We won't have to wash the plates," the girls said. "That way, we'll save water."

"There is something else to think about," said Tara's mother. "Paper is made from trees. Using paper plates means more trees have to be cut down."

"Why is that important?" asked one of the girls.

"Trees help to clean the air," Tara's mother explained. "We need trees to help fight air pollution."

Tara and her friends knew about air pollution. They lived in a town called El Segundo, in southern California. Some days, the sky turned a dirty brown. Sometimes the air had a bad smell.

El Segundo is near busy freeways. Car engines are a big cause of air pollution. Los Angeles International Airport is also close by. Airplanes burn lots of fuel when they take off. They cause air pollution, too. Factories nearby sent smoke into the air. That made the problem even worse.

"It isn't good to breathe air pollution," Tara and her friends agreed. "But what can a bunch of third graders do about it?"

A Huge Oil Spill

It was just after midnight on March 24, 1989. A huge oil tanker moved slowly through the waters off the coast of Alaska. The tanker was almost as long as 10 football fields.

The oil tanker was called the *Exxon Valdez*. That night, it carried more than 53 million gallons of oil.

Suddenly, disaster struck. The ship's pilot became tired or careless. He steered the tanker out of the safe sea-lanes. The ship ran straight into a reef that lay under the water.

The reef punched a huge hole in the ship. Oil began leaking into the water.

Over the next few days, more than 10 million gallons of oil spread through the water. Birds and other animals got covered in oil. The oil ruined their feathers and fur. They couldn't stay warm. Some of them began to freeze to death.

As the creatures tried to clean themselves, they swallowed some of the oil. The oil poisoned many of them.

People in Alaska were worried and angry. Thick, sticky oil coated more than 1,100 miles of the Alaska shore. Many thousands of birds and other animals were sick and dying.

"What can we do about this?" people asked. "And how can we make sure it never happens again?"

Stopping Oil Spills

After the oil spill, people did their best to clean up the mess. Rescuers rushed to save birds and other animals. Thousands of workers began trying to clean up the water and beaches.

But nothing could ever solve all the problems caused by the *Exxon Valdez*. The spill killed more than 250,000 seabirds. About 3,000 otters died. So did 300 seals and 22 killer whales. Some types of animals have still not recovered. You can still find oil from the *Exxon Valdez* on some beaches today.

The best solution to big oil spills is to stop them from happening. So, our government has tried to make sure that companies and their workers act more safely.

The government made the company that owned the *Exxon Valdez* pay hundreds of millions of dollars in fines. Some of the money helped to pay for the cleanup. Some of it was a punishment for the company.

The ship's captain was punished, too. He had to pay 50 thousand dollars. He also had to spend many hours helping the people of the community.

The government also passed laws to make oil shipping safer. For example, oil tankers in Alaska now must have stronger hulls.

Communities in Alaska have tried to become more prepared in case another big spill happens. But everyone hopes it never does.

Schools and Toxic Waste

Kim grew up in Marion, Ohio. When she was 28, she became very sick. Her doctors said she had a rare type of cancer.

A few years later, other people in town started getting cancer. All of them had gone to River Valley High School.

Some people in Marion began to wonder why so many people in their town had cancer. They wondered if something in the high school was causing students to get sick.

Kim's parents joined a group called Concerned River Valley Families. The group demanded that scientists test the school grounds.

It turned out that the ground under the high school contained **toxic waste**. Toxic means

poisonous. Waste is something that is left over or thrown away.

The toxic waste in Marion came from the United States Army. Years before, the army had used the land as a place to dump chemicals. The school was built right on top of the toxic waste dump.

The army said the land was safe. So did the government of Ohio. The scientists said, "You can't blame the toxic waste for the cancers. We don't know what causes Kim's type of cancer."

The Concerned Families disagreed. They said, "We can't take chances with our children's health. The school is not safe!"

Making Sure Schools Are Safe

The Concerned River Valley Families wanted to close the high school. They talked to the people in charge of the school. They went to public meetings. They made sure that news reporters wrote about the problem.

Thanks to these families, the River Valley story made news around the country. Lois Gibbs even came to visit. Do you remember her? She was the mother who spoke up about the dangerous chemicals at Love Canal.

In the end, the families didn't win their fight. River Valley High School stayed open. But the people of Marion voted to build a new school in another location.

Did toxic waste cause Kim and other students to get cancer? No one knows for sure. But many scientists say that toxic waste is especially dangerous for growing children. For this reason, communities should make very sure that schools are safe.

Around the country, concerned parents are taking action. They have stopped some schools from being built on old garbage dumps. And they have worked to close schools where dangerous chemicals have been found.

These parents have learned an important lesson. It is the same lesson that Tara Church and the Tree Musketeers learned. Pollution is a problem that affects everyone. And everyone can be part of the solution.

Wrap-Up

Solving pollution problems is up to all of us. A few girls in California planted trees to help solve air pollution. People in Alaska helped to solve a water pollution problem by passing laws. One mother spread the word about polluted schools to help end this problem. What might you do to help solve a pollution problem?

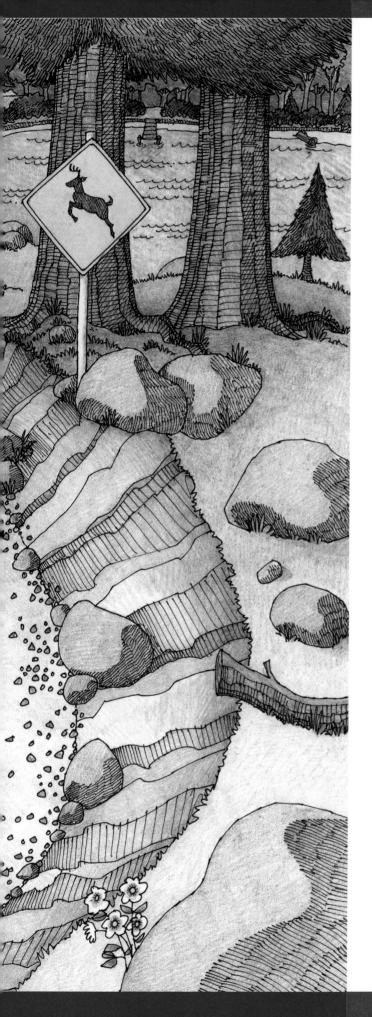

14

How Can We Help the Global Community?

We are all part of many communities. Some communities are small, like your school. Others are much bigger, like your state. The largest community of all is the **global community**. All of us are members of this community. So are animals and other living things. We all share our planet's water, air, and soil. We all depend on each other to have healthy and happy lives.

It's up to us to take care of the global community. This chapter has lots of ideas for ways to share our Earth. How many others can you think of?

Protect the Environment

In Chapter 13, you learned about some ways that people have tried to protect the environment. Here are some things you can do.

Help Fight Air Pollution

Cars are a major cause of air pollution. A good way to fight air pollution is to cut down on how much we drive.

Often, there's another way to get where you want to go. Instead of riding in a car, you could take a bus, a train, or a subway. Or, you could ride your bike or walk.

Still need a car to get places? Try to find other people who are going to the same place, and ride together in one car.

Help Reduce Waste

The average American throws away four pounds of garbage every day! All that garbage gets dumped in landfills. Someday, we will run out of places to put our trash.

Most towns and cities have recycling programs. Recycling means using things over again. You can recycle cans, bottles, newspapers, and other things. You may even be able to recycle used batteries.

Reducing and reusing are ways to create less waste in the first place. Reducing means to make

less trash. For example, buying a large box of cereal will mean less cardboard to recycle than buying several smaller boxes. Reusing means to use things more than once. For example, you might use both sides of a sheet of paper before recycling it. Some artists make art from things that other people have thrown away.

Help Save Energy and Water

Using fewer resources, such as oil and water, helps the environment. Energy uses up resources that can never be replaced. Even fresh water will become scarce in the future. You can help by saving precious energy and water.

Use energy wisely. Turn off the lights when you leave a room. Turn off televisions, stereos, and computers when no one is using them. In cold weather, turn down the heat and wear a sweater.

Americans waste huge amounts of water. But, there are many ways to waste less water. Try taking shorter showers. Don't leave the water running when you brush your teeth. When you help wash the family car, use a sprayer you can turn off when you lay the hose down. Tell your school or city about sprinklers that are broken or are watering the sidewalk instead of the lawn.

Protect Wildlife

We share the planet with many kinds of wildlife. Birds and other animals need our protection to survive.

Help Keep Animals Safe

People have put many kinds of wildlife in danger. Here are three ways you can help keep animals safe.

Buy dolphin-safe tuna. The nets used for tuna fishing have trapped and killed hundreds of dolphins. Wise fishermen use nets that allow dolphins to escape. You can help by buying tuna that says "dolphin safe" on the label.

Avoid buying things made from endangered animals. Some examples are things made with ivory, fur, shells, and alligator skins.

Find out about dangers to wildlife in your area. Some lawn fertilizers are poisonous to birds. Help make your own backyard a safer place for animals and wildlife.

Help Save Animal Habitats

Habitats are places where animals live. You can protect animals by helping to save their homes.

First, you can protect local habitats. We often spoil animal habitats with our trash. For example, many birds and other animals get tangled in the plastic rings from soft-drink packaging. Others choke on old balloons and other litter. Don't be a litterbug! Even better, take along a trash bag when you visit a park or a beach. Help the animals by picking up other people's litter.

You can also support wildlife groups. Lots of groups are working to save animal habitats around the world. You can find many of these groups on the Internet. Some even have kids' clubs you can join.

Help Other People

People in friendly communities help each other. We can all do something to help others.

Share with People in Need

Sometimes people can't afford basic things such as clothing and food. You can help by sharing what you have.

Don't throw away those old clothes! Instead, donate them to community groups that share good used clothing with people who need it.

Other groups collect food for families in need. You've probably seen collection barrels at your supermarket, especially around the holidays. Don't pass them by! You might give up buying a snack for yourself so your family can make a donation. You might even donate extra food you find in your own kitchen cabinets.

Lend a Helping Hand

Many groups get people together to help others. Look for a group that's right for you.

One such group, UNICEF, helps needy children around the world. Every Halloween, thousands of kids trick-or-treat to collect money for UNICEF instead of candy for themselves.

A town in California has a group called Kids Cheering Kids. These kids give some of their free time to help other kids. They visit sick children in hospitals. They help students with schoolwork. They spend time with children in homeless shelters. If you can't find a group like this to join, maybe you can start one!

Treat Others with Respect

Everyone needs respect and kindness. You can make a big difference just by how you act toward other people.

Being **tolerant** means respecting people even if they're different from you. It's hurtful to make fun of others or to harm them because of the way they look, dress, or talk. If you see people acting this way, speak up. Remind them that everyone deserves respect.

Take time to learn about other people. The more you know about others, the more you will respect them. Talk to new people in your school or town. You might even try being pen pals with a child in another country!

Wrap-Up

We are all members of the global community. Each one of us can help make our world a better place. We can help protect the environment. We can help protect wildlife. We can help other people.

United States Political Map

152

United States Physical Map

130°   125°   120°   115°   110°   105°   100°

50°

Lake Winnipegosis   Lake Winnipeg

Vancouver Island

C A

Lake Manitoba

C. Flattery

WASHINGTON

45°

Mt. Rainier ▲

Columbia

Missouri

MONTANA

NORTH DAKOTA

Missouri

James

OREGON

IDAHO

Snake

WYOMING

SOUTH DAKOTA

R   O   C   K   Y

C A S C A D E   R A N G E

Klamath

40°
C. Mendocino

Sacramento

Great Salt Lake

Redwood

N. Platte

NEBRASKA

S. Platte

NEVADA

UTAH

Colorado

Mt. Elbert ▲

KANSAS

S I E R R A   N E V A D A

▲ Mt. Whitney

COLORADO

Arkansas

35°

CALIFORNIA

Cimarron

OKL

Pt. Arguello

Colorado

ARIZONA

NEW MEXICO

Canadian

CHANNEL ISLANDS

Gila

Rio Grande

Red

30°

GULF OF SANTA CATALINA

Pecos

TEXAS

Bi

160°   159°   158°   157°   156°   155°

Mt. ▲
22°   Kawaikini   KAUAI   22°

NIIHAU   OAHU

Kauai Channel   MOLOKAI

21°   21°

MAUI
▲ Kolekole

LANAI
KAHOOLAWE   HAWAII

20°   20°
P A C I F I C   O C E A N   Mauna Kea

Keahole Point

▲ Mauna Loa

0   50   100   150 miles
0   50   100   150   200 kilometers

Conic projection

19°   19°

159°   158°   157°   156°   155°

115°

170°   160°   150°

ARCTIC OCEAN   ARCTIC COASTAL PLAIN

CHUKCHI SEA   Colville   140°

Kotzebue Sound   Noatak   BROOKS RANGE

Kobuk   Koyukuk

Bering Strait Strait

Norton Sound   Yukon   Yukon

St. Lawrence Island   Tanana

ALASKA

Mt. McKinley ▲ A L A S K A
Susitna

Nunivak Island   Illiamna Lake

Mt. Bona ▲ ▲ Mt. Logan

ALEXANDER ARCHIPELAGO

Cape Newenham

BRISTOL BAY   GULF OF ALASKA

QUEEN CHARLOTTE ISLANDS

Kodiak Island

Trinity Islands
Chirikov Island

Unimak Island   Shumagin Islands

0   500 miles
0   500 kilometers

Conical orthomorphic projection

170°   160°   150°   140°

MEXICO

Rio Grande

100°

154

CANADA

MINNESOTA

WISCONSIN

Lake Nipigon

Lake Superior

Georgian Bay

Lake Michigan

Lake Huron

MICHIGAN

Lake Ontario

Lake Erie

James Bay

GULF OF ST. LAWRENCE

Prince Edward Island

Nova Scotia

MAINE

Cape Sable

VERMONT

NEW HAMPSHIRE

MASSACHUSETTS

Cape Cod

RHODE ISLAND

CONNECTICUT

NEW YORK

PENNSYLVANIA

NEW JERSEY

IOWA

ILLINOIS

INDIANA

OHIO

WASHINGTON D.C.

WEST VIRGINIA

Ohio

VIRGINIA

Delaware Bay

DELAWARE

MARYLAND

Chesapeake Bay

ATLANTIC OCEAN

Mississippi

Missouri

MISSOURI

KENTUCKY

TENNESSEE

Cape Hatteras

Bermuda

NORTH CAROLINA

ARKANSAS

Arkansas

Tennessee

APPALACHIAN MOUNTAINS

SOUTH CAROLINA

Cape Fear

OKLAHOMA

MISSISSIPPI ALABAMA

Alabama

GEORGIA

N
W E
S

LOUISIANA

Mississippi

Mississippi Delta

Cape Canaveral

FLORIDA

Lake Okeechobee

Grand Bahama Island

BAHAMAS

Tropic of Cancer

GULF OF MEXICO

Andros Island

TURKS & CAICOS ISLANDS

Florida Keys

Straits of Florida

Great Inagua Island

CUBA

Lambert's equal-area projection

0   500 miles

0   500 kilometers

155

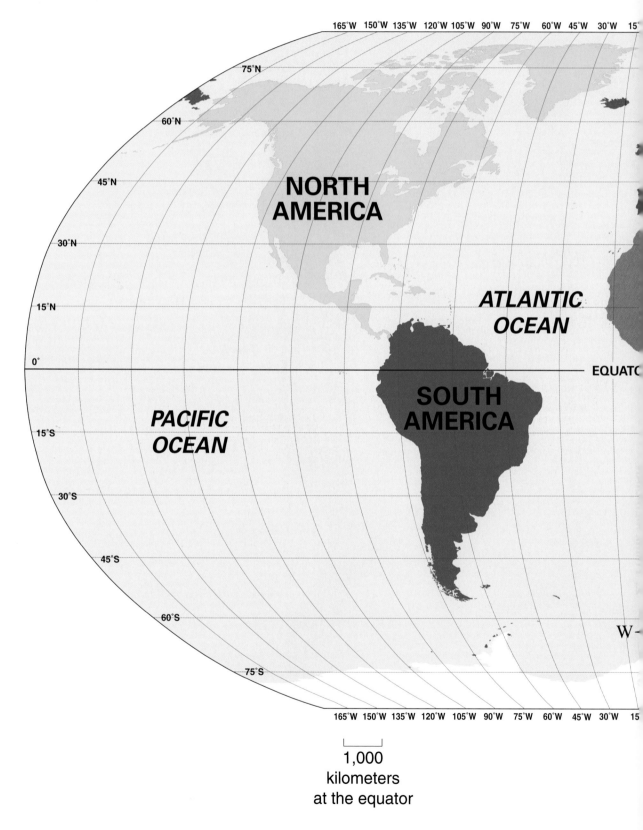

1,000
kilometers
at the equator

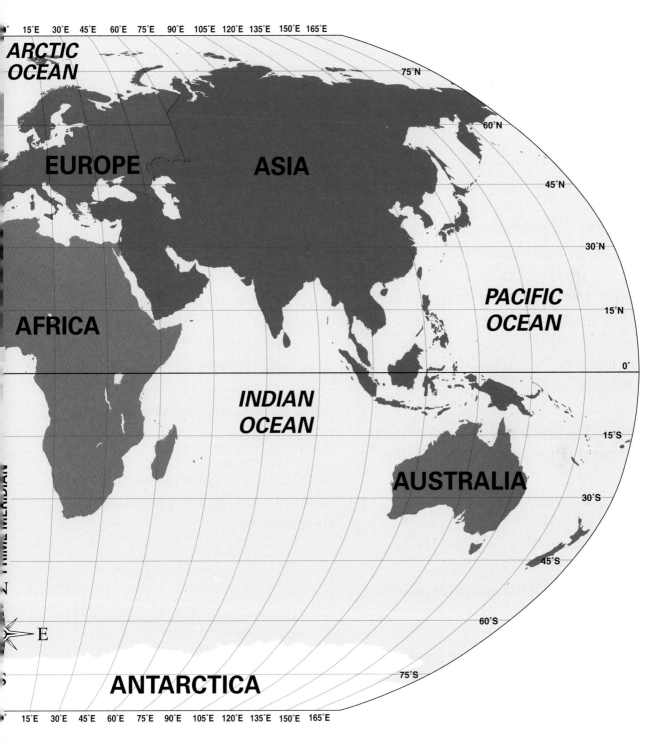

15°E 30°E 45°E 60°E 75°E 90°E 105°E 120°E 135°E 150°E 165°E

ARCTIC OCEAN

EUROPE

ASIA

75°N

60°N

45°N

30°N

AFRICA

PACIFIC OCEAN

15°N

0°

INDIAN OCEAN

15°S

AUSTRALIA

30°S

45°S

E

60°S

ANTARCTICA

75°S

15°E 30°E 45°E 60°E 75°E 90°E 105°E 120°E 135°E 150°E 165°E

Robinson Projecton

Glossary

B

ballot a piece of paper on which people mark their votes in an election

budget a plan for how to use money

C

canal a waterway made by humans

candidate a person who wants to be elected to do a job for the community

cardinal directions the four main points on a compass: north, south, east, and west

city a community that has lots of buildings and people

city hall the building where the offices of a community's government are located

climate the weather in a place

con a negative thing

continent one of the seven large bodies of land on Earth

country an area of land with its own government

culture a way of life shared by a group of people

D

demand the total amount of a product that customers are willing to buy at a certain price

demonstration a gathering of people to show shared feelings or opinions

disabled not able to do things, like walk or talk, without help

discriminate to treat someone unfairly

diverse made up of different groups of people

E

economy how things are bought and sold in a community

equator the imaginary line that divides Earth into the Northern and Southern Hemispheres

F

fare the price charged for using public transportation

farmworker someone who works on a farm

G

geography the study of Earth's surface

global community the community made up of all the people on Earth

global trade the buying and selling of goods around the world

government the people and work that keep a community running smoothly

H

habitat a place where animals and plants live

hemisphere half of a sphere, such as a half of the planet Earth

I

immigrant a person who leaves one country to live in another

L

law a rule in a community that tells people what they can and cannot do

M

manufacture to use machines to make something, such as a car or a computer

market any place where buyers and sellers come together

N

natural resource an item that comes from nature, such as fish, trees, and water

O

ocean one of the four largest bodies of water on Earth

P

peaceful done without hurting others

physical geography the features of Earth's surface, like mountains, plains, lakes, and rivers

pollution anything that harms the air, water, or soil

prime meridian the imaginary line that divides Earth into the Eastern and Western Hemispheres

pro a positive thing

public service a service or job that all members of a community can use, such as a public library

public works construction projects that help everyone in a community, like streets, parks, and bridges

S

sphere an object that is shaped like a ball

state a smaller part of a country; the United States has 50 states

streetcar small trains that use city streets

strike when workers stop working until people help fix their problems

subway a train that runs under the ground

supply the total amount of a product for sale

T

tolerant respectful of other people

town a community with buildings and people that is smaller than a city

toxic waste trash or garbage that hurts people and the environment

tradition something that people do together year after year

V

volunteer a person who does a service and receives no pay for it, such as a volunteer firefighter

Credits

Contents

Chapter 1

2-3, Rosiland Solomon; **4**, Corbis; **7**, © 2002 Micheal Simpson/Getty Images/FPG; **8, upper**, © 2002 M-Sat/Getty Images/FPG; **10**, courtesy of NASA

Chapter 2

12-13, Doug Roy; **17, lower**, © Digital Vision Ltd.; **18, lower**, Corbis; **19, upper**, © Digital Vision Ltd.

Chapter 3

20-21, Rosiland Solomon; **22**, Doug Roy; **24**, courtesy of Airgems, Kitty and Terry Miller; **25, upper**, Corbis; **25, lower**, Corbis; **26**, Corbis; **29, upper right**, © 2002 Arnulf Husmo/Getty Images/Stone; **29, lower right**, Corbis

Chapter 4

30-31, Len Ebert; **32**, Corbis; **33**, Corbis; **34, upper**, Corbis; **35**, Corbis; **36**, Corbis; **37, left**, Corbis; **37, right**, Corbis

Chapter 5

38-39, DJ Simison; **40**, © 2002 Miao China Tourism Press.Wang/Getty Images/The Image Bank; **41, upper**, Corbis; **41, lower**, Corbis; **42, upper**, Corbis; **42, lower**, Corbis; **43**, Corbis; **44, upper**, © 2002 Tom Wilson/Getty Images/FPG; **44, lower**, Corbis; **45**, Corbis; **46**, © 2002 Andy Sacks/Getty Images/Stone; **47**, © 2002 Lori Adamski Peek/Getty Images/Stone

Chapter 6

48-49, DJ Simison; **50**, Corbis; **51**, Corbis; **52**, Corbis; **53**, © 2002 Jim Cummins/Getty Images/FPG; **54**, Corbis; **55**, Corbis; **56**, © F. Pedrick/The Image Works; **57**, © 2002 Jim Cummins/Getty Images/FPG

Chapter 7

58-59, Len Ebert; **60, lower**, Corbis; **61**, © 2002 Lawrence Migdale/Getty Images/Stone; **62, lower right**, courtesy of Charles Shafsky; **62, lower left**, courtesy of Charles Shafsky; **63**, courtesy of Charles Shafsky; **64, lower**, © 2002 Charles Gupton/Getty Images/Stone; **65**, Corbis; **66, lower**, © 2002 National Geographic Image Collection/Raymond K. Gehman; **67**, Corbis; **68, lower**, Corbis; **69**, Corbis; **70, lower**, Corbis; **71**, Corbis

Chapter 8

72-73, Susan Jaekel; **74**, Corbis; **75, lower**, Corbis; **76**, Corbis; **77**, Corbis; **80**, Corbis; **81**, © 2002 Michael Melford/Getty Images/The Image Bank

Chapter 9

82-83, Doug Roy; **84**, Corbis; **85**, Corbis; **86**, Corbis; **87**, Corbis; **88**, Corbis; **89**, Corbis; **91**, Corbis

Chapter 10

92-93, Renata Lohman; **94**, Corbis; **95, lower**, Corbis; **96**, © 2002 Weinberg.Clark/Getty Images/The Image Bank; **97**, © 2002 Richard Price/Getty Images/FPG; **98**, Corbis; **99, left**, Corbis; **99, right**, © 2002 Keren Su/Getty Images/FPG; **101**, Corbis; **102**, Corbis; **103, left**, Corbis; **103, right**, Corbis; **104**, Corbis; **105**, Corbis

Chapter 11

106-107, Len Ebert; **108,** Corbis; **109,** Corbis; **110,** © 2002 Michael Malyszko/Getty Images/ FPG; **111,** © 2002 Peter Cade/Getty Images/ The Image Bank; **112,** Corbis; **113,** Corbis; **114,** © 2002 Bob Peterson/Getty Images/FPG; **115,** © 2002 Ron Chapple/Getty Images/FPG; **117,** Corbis

Chapter 12

118-119, Jane McCreary; **121,** Corbis; **122,** Corbis; **123,** Corbis; **124,** Corbis; **125,** Corbis; **126,** © 2002 Jonathan Nourok/Getty Images/ Stone; **127,** © 2002 Andy Sacks/Getty Images/ Stone

Chapter 13

128-129, Jane McCreary; **132,** © 2002 Lori Adamski Peek/Getty Images/Stone; **133, upper,** courtesy of Tree Musketeers, El Segundo, California; **133, lower,** courtesy of Tree Musketeers, El Segundo, California; **134,** Corbis; **134,** Corbis; **135,** Corbis; **136,** © 2002 Ben Osborne/Getty Images/Stone; **137,** Corbis; **139,** © 2002 Rich Frishman/ Getty Images/Stone; **141,** © 2002 Rob Brimson/Getty Images/FPG

Chapter 14

142-143, Doug Roy; **146,** © 2002 Andy Sacks/ Getty Images/Stone; **148,** © 2002 Arthur Tilley/Getty Images/FPG; **149,** Corbis; **150,** Corbis